Online business ideas for fast sales

Expanding on the web deals is the essential objective of incalculable organizations, huge and little similar. Whether you run a mother-and-pop retail business or work for a tremendous internet business goliath like Amazon, expanding deals through web-based channels is similar to bowling a strike - it looks much simpler than it really is.

Chris Moen

Copyright ©

Table of contents

Introduction

Chapter one

Introduction

Luckily, there are many ways you can make more deals on the web, a considerable lot of which you can carry out immediately. A portion of these tips center around unambiguous techniques you can execute, while others are more summed up. Here, we'll be taking a gander at 25 such procedures, so whether you sell actual products or maintain a help based business, the following are 25 noteworthy strategies you can use to increment online deals execution.

Chapter one

1. Be Honest in Your Sales Copy

This could appear to be agonizingly self-evident, yet it's astonishing to me the number of destinations that compose checks their items can't cash. In addition to the fact that honesty is critical to your business' standing, it likewise cultivates and empowers trust in your image. Try not to make claims you can't validate, and don't utilize poetic exaggeration gently - the present buyers are easily affected to promoting BS, so tell the truth, direct, and congenial in the entirety of your deals duplicate, from your landing page to your email crusades.

This guideline likewise applies to how you position yourself as a business. At any point go over a site that is clearly shown to a couple of individuals, but includes duplicates that could be more qualified to a global venture organization? This approach not just makes you look stupid, it additionally harms your image's validity. Assuming you're a little organization, invest wholeheartedly in that and be forthright about it - numerous purchasers are going to more modest organizations exactly in light of the more individualized, individual help they can offer. Try not to attempt to be something you're not.

2. Get More Ad Clicks with Ad Extensions

In the event that you're selling stuff on the web, promotion expansions are an easy decision - this element (accessible in both AdWords and Bing) permits you to make your advertisement greater with additional spots to click. What's more, it costs no extra! What's more, it builds your promotion's active clicking factor! Astonishing, correct?

```
Ray-Ban® Sunglasses - Free Shipping & Returns
www.ray-ban.com/Sunglasses
Shop Ray-Ban® Sunglasses Online
#Campaign4Change · Virtual Mirror · Online Exclusives · Customize With REMIX
Styles: Aviator, Wayfarer, Clubmaster, Round, Custom
Ratings: Shipping 9.5/10 · Website 9/10 · Quality 9/10 · Selection 8.5/10
    Men's Sunglasses              Women's Sunglasses
    Discover The Latest Collection For    Check Out The Latest Women's
    Men Plus Get Free Shipping            Styles And Trends For Any Occasion
```

In the above model, the connections to "Men's Sunglasses" and "Ladies' Sunglasses" give individuals who are hoping to purchase another set of Ray-Ban's two extra places to click. This saves the potential client a stage and makes it simpler and quicker to find precisely the exact thing they need (so they go to your site rather than a contender's).

3. Flaunt Customer Testimonials and Trust Signals

In the present online entertainment climate, client criticism has never been more significant. Luckily, this implies that your fulfilled clients can give you quite possibly the most significant weapon in your stockpile - tributes.

Armies of fulfilled clients are significantly more persuasive than even the best-composed deals duplicate, so ensure you incorporate spouting tributes and surveys from your bad-to-the-bone brand evangelists spouting about how magnificent you are. These could show up on your item pages, points of arrival, valuing page, even your landing page. For more data, look at my post on the force of client tributes.

Essentially, the consideration of trust signs can be a great method for expanding on the web deals as well as normal request esteem, as it makes a better impression of your image in the brain of the possibility and might possibly defeat delays prudently. Assuming that your business has any expert licenses (even something as normal as a Better Business Bureau certificate or participation in your neighborhood office of trade), put these trust signals up front on your site. In the event that you have a great rundown of fulfilled clients, ensure your possibilities are familiar.

4. Make a Sense of Urgency

It's vital to tell the truth and straightforward about what your identity is and what you do, yet there's no standard against making a need to get going to convince possibilities to purchase from you at this moment.

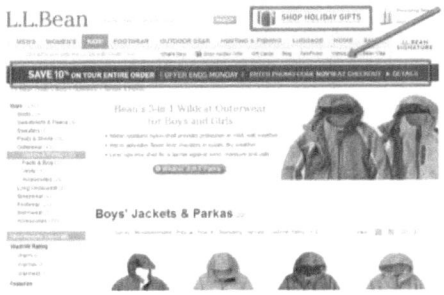

Numerous customers answer emphatically to motivators that make a need to get going, from time-delicate extraordinary proposals to restricted release items. Albeit the manners in which you can achieve this are essentially as different as the items you can purchase on the web, a few procedures might be more successful than others. For instance, in the event that you don't (or can't) make a restricted release item to tempt possibilities, perhaps you can offer a monetary motivation to clients who focus on a buy immediately, like free delivery or a rebate.

In AdWords, you can utilize promotion customizers to show a commencement on an occasional proposition or restricted time deal:

```
50+ LCD TVs on Sale              50+ LCD TVs on Sale
www.buytvs.com                   www.buytvs.com
30% Off LCDs. Sale ends in 4 hours.   30% Off LCDs. Sale ends in 1 hour.
Ships free in the US. Shop Now!  Ships free in the US. Shop Now!
```

Anyway you decide to make it happen, making a need to get moving is an incredible method for expanding on the web.

5. Offer a Bulletproof Money-Back Guarantee

Regularly, perhaps of the most impressive calculation, a shopper's choice not to purchase something is hazard avoidance - the longing to stay away from a possible misfortune. Most times, this apparent gamble is a monetary one. For what reason would it be advisable for someone to purchase your items? Imagine a scenario in which they don't work, or the client could do without them. Indeed, even little buys can convey the gamble of "purchaser's regret," so beat this protest from the very beginning by offering an impenetrable unconditional promise.

The more gamble you eliminate from the possibility's choice, the more probable they are to purchase from you, so remove whatever might deter possibilities from purchasing from you.

7. Target Lookalike Audiences on Facebook

One of the most incredible ways of expanding on the web deals is to utilize the information you have about your current clients to find individuals very much like them. Facebook permits you to do this through the focusing of carbon copy crowds.

Carbon copy crowds in Facebook are basically clients on Facebook who share attributes and ways of behaving to clients in your data set. You transfer your information to Facebook, which then, at that point, cross-references its own information (and data from outsider information merchants) to make matches in light of the measures you determine. You can likewise utilize following pixels and information from application establishments to assist you with making carbon copy crowds. This is a brilliant method for making the information on your current clients work for you, as it really permits you to extraordinarily grow your scope with negligible exertion and utilize profoundly designated advertisements to allure Facebook clients who are basically the same as your current clients.

8. Decrease Friction in the Checkout Process
As per Business Insider, roughly $4 TRILLION worth of online product was deserted in deficient shopping baskets last year alone, of which 63% was possibly recoverable. This is a genuinely stunning measurement, and one that uncovers that it is so critical to nail your checkout interaction.

Like the point above about client experience, diminishing grating in your checkout cycle can amazingly affect your transformation rates. Similarly as you ought to make it as simple as workable for guests to utilize and explore your site, you ought to make it much more straightforward for them to really purchase what you're selling.

Wipe out any pointless strides in your checkout cycle that could deter a possibility from changing over. Skirt superfluous fields in structures. Try not to time them out and make them begin once again all along.

9. Give however many Payment Options as could reasonably be expected

OK, so your business assumes praise cards. And Google Wallet installments? Or on the other hand ApplePay? And Stripe? WePay?

Buyers have more decisions than any time in recent memory as far as how they really pay for labor and products, and not every person likes to utilize American Express. By offering greater installment choices, including fresher administrations that are turning out to be progressively famous on portable devices, you're making it simpler for people to give you their cash. Of course, it tends to be a problem to enhance your website (and checkout process, as we examined above) to incorporate this large number of choices, yet doing so is an extraordinary method for expanding on the web deals, especially in the event that your website has solid portable traffic.

On a connected note, site security is central, especially for internet business destinations where guests are giving installment data. The most ideal way to get your site is with a SSL declaration. The cycle, evaluating, and kind of authentication you really want changes relying upon the size of your site and your industry and the supplier you pick. A few deal them free of charge however require ordinary recharging, a few offer them as a paid yet once choice, while others offer them free as a component of a bigger contribution. For instance, HubSpot incorporates free SSL encryption with its CMS.

10. Put resources into Quality Product Images
There's indisputable proof that first rate food really tastes better compared to carelessly plated dishes. Considering how significant appearance is compared to how we see things (counting others), it makes sense that putting resources into quality item photography will likewise affect guests to your site.

Despite what you sell, incorporate great pictures of your items - no small thumbnails or dim shots taken in your stockroom. Likewise make certain to incorporate a large number of pictures. It could appear pointless to incorporate shots of your items from each possible point, yet give it a shot. Individuals love to kick an item's supposed tires prior to purchasing, particularly on the web.

11. Dispose of Your Landing Pages

We've referenced this methodology previously, and it ordinarily raises in excess of a couple of eyebrows without a doubt. Nonetheless, we're not pushing for disposing of presentation pages superfluously, but instead improving your internet based promotions to line up with the number of buyers that really peruse the Web and shop on the web.

Call-Only missions in Facebook and AdWords are a magnificent illustration of a circumstance where eliminating the conventional greeting page seems OK. The vast majority would rather not endure a few minutes perusing pages on their cell phone - they basically need to reach out to your business.

By using Call-Only advertisements, you're making it more straightforward for possibilities to contact your business, killing one of the leakiest phases of the exemplary web-based deals pipe totally, and possibly expanding the volume of calls to your business - one of the most significant lead sources to numerous organizations. Individuals who call you are for all intents and purposes beseeching you to sell them something.

12. Check Gmail Ads Out

After years all through beta, Gmail Ads are FINALLY accessible to everybody. This is a thrilling method for arriving at possibilities and incremental deals.

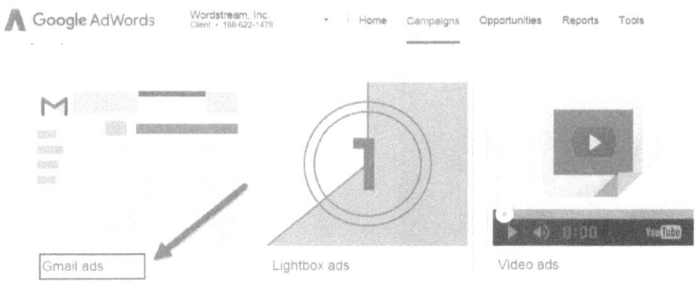

Assuming you're now arriving at clients when they search and when they peruse on friendly terms, why not exceed all expectations and hit them while they're in their inboxes, as well? One of the best ways of utilizing Gmail Ads is by focusing on contender catchphrases. Individuals who are on the lookout for your rivals' items are receiving messages from your rivals that notice their image terms at the present time. By focusing on those equivalent terms you can appear in their inboxes and ideally adjust their perspectives.

13. Continue To message Consistent Across Campaigns and Your Site
At any point clicked a PPC promotion that caught your eye, just to be taken to an insignificant greeting page (terrible) or the site's landing page (more regrettable)? Did you wind up purchasing anything you were searching for from that site? Most likely not.

A presentation promotion for Air Canada, and it's going with a greeting page.

Assuming that a client clicks a promotion for a particular item or administration, the page they're taken to ought to be about that particular item or administration - not a connected classification, not an exceptional proposal for another item, but rather that particular item. Ensure your information is applicable across your PPC and paid social missions and the pages related with them, so that promotion clicks really transform into deals.

14. Answer Every Question and Address Every Objection in Your Copy

Quite possibly the most risky trap you can fall into while attempting to sell online is making presumptions about your imminent clients' information on your item, administration, or even market. Many organizations erroneously accept their clients find out about the thing they're selling than they really do, which brings about unanswered inquiries or complaints that are neglected to be tended to - the two of which can hurt deals.

Consider each question you might potentially consider about your item, and respond to it in your duplicate on your item pages. Essentially, contemplate each potential complaint a possibility could have about your contribution, and prudently beat it in your duplicate. This could appear to be illogical, yet recollect that, you're not assaulting possibilities with pointless data - you're giving them precisely what they need to settle on an educated choice. This approach is likewise a great practice recorded as a hard copy, tight, clear, brief duplicate. In the event that you're concerned there's a lot of duplication, you can continuously manage it down. Simply maintain the emphasis on the client and how it benefits them, not why your organization is so wonderful.

15. Offer As Much As You Possibly Can for Free

Individuals love free stuff, and the more you offer for nothing, the more likely clients are going to see you and your image, which can bring about additional internet based deals.

Magnificent!

Check your ongoing contributions out. Could you at any point offer anything free of charge? On the off chance that you're in the product business as we are, sans offering, no-commitment preliminaries of your software is simple. Or then again even free devices like ROI number crunchers and other intelligent substances (Outgrow is an incredible instrument for this!).

Regardless of whether you're not, you can straightforwardly offer samplers, preliminary enrollments, two-for-one offers, and other award-based motivations. Offering stuff for nothing isn't simply an incredible method for working on individuals' impression of your business, it's likewise an extraordinary method for acquainting them with your priority items and enticing them to purchase more.

16. Make and Target Detailed Buyer Personas
I'm feeling free to expect that you're as of now making purchaser personas (since, supposing that you're not, you're in genuine difficulty), yet I will provoke you to make much more definite purchaser personas than you have previously.

Assuming you've at any point taken a gander at the focusing on choices accessible to Facebook promoters, you might have seen the astonishing granularity with which you can target clients on Facebook - publicists can target clients in view of the area of their home, the college from which they procured their certificate, and even where they anticipate going for their next excursion.

Clearly, this level of explicitness might be a just a tad ridiculous over the top excess for your purchaser personas, yet the better you "know" your ideal clients, the more probable they are to answer painstakingly created information custom-made explicitly to their lives. Drive yourself to make more itemized purchaser personas than you ever have previously.

17. Execute Tiered Pricing

At the point when you go to a café, the odds are very great that you'll constantly pick one of the mid-evaluated dishes. This is on the grounds that numerous cafés control brain research to push individuals toward mid-range dinners. We'll frequently stay away from the least expensive dishes - and the most costly - making the center level choices the most engaging. This is a method known as "bait evaluating." A similar rule can be utilized to increment deals online with layered estimating structures.

By including a third "distraction" choice in your estimating structure, you can push individuals close to the center choice - the one you truly maintain that they should purchase. Indeed, certain individuals will go for the most costly choice at any rate (which is a reward, income wise), however most will subliminally keep away from the distraction and pick the center level choice, which is unequivocally what you maintain that they should do.

Many organizations influence this mental standard (otherwise called the "unbalanced predominance impact") to make us purchase what they need.

18. Add an Opt-In Pop-Up Offer to Push Them Over the Edge

Assuming you're hoping to increase deals in retail, don't disregard the capability of pick in offers - prompts that urge individuals to pursue your bulletin, mailing rundown, or steadfastness programs. Utilizing select in offers can not just essentially increment the quantity of contacts in your data set (a significant resource for future email showcasing efforts), yet additionally increment online deals for the time being.

Planned clients who are vacillating about purchasing from you likely could be influenced by a very much positioned selection in offer for, say, free delivery, or 10% of their most memorable request. Regardless of whether they rule against the buy around then, however pursue your selection on offer, you've actually added them to your data set and they might decide to return later to finish the deal.

While sending off a select in offer, make certain to test each component for greatest advancement. Test the start of the duplicate, the situation at which it shows up on your site, and the stream that guests are coordinated through the interaction. A/B test various offers and see which ones yield a more noteworthy volume of recruits. Consider having the spring up be set off by a site exit so guests see it not long before they're about the leave the page. The more individuals that pursue your bulletin or reliability program, the more potential deals you can make from here on out.

19. Develop Online Sales with Mobile Optimization

The quantity of web-based organizations with ineffectively planned, gravely upgraded "portable" locales is astounding.

Portable pursuit has previously overshadowed work area search in volume. To overlook deals, it's indispensable that your site is enhanced for portable use - and not simply according to a specialized viewpoint.

Make it as simple as feasible for portable guests to purchase anything you're selling. This might include a broad update of your checkout interaction (see tip #18), or the plan and send off of a completely different portable site. Amazon's portable site is a superb illustration of how versatile web-based business can (and seemingly ought to) be finished, yet you needn't bother with Amazon's assets to make a convincing, easy to understand insight for guests on portable.

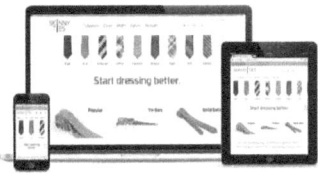

Route and client experience are among the most significant components of a planned, profoundly improved versatile experience. The harder it is for guests to find - and purchase - what they need, the almost certain they are to leave your site by and large and take their business somewhere else. Pages ought to stack close promptly, and routes ought to be intelligent. Try not to request an excess of data, just the absolute minimum you really want to either make the deal or market to possibilities later. Permit guests to return to their trucks later, even on another gadget. Try not to anticipate that portable guests should change over in a solitary meeting, since they presumably (certainly) will not - however they could change over later, assuming you make it simple for them to do as such.

Consider your portable guests and do all that you can to make it easy for them to purchase from you while they're in a hurry.

20. Dazzle New Customers with an Amazing Follow-Up Email

Tragically, the client experience commonly ends for some organizations when they've at last got their hands on a client's cash. This is a horrible mix-up for client maintenance. To increase deals volume on the web, ensure you have a smart, kind, truly helpful subsequent strategy set up for new clients.

As a no-nonsense PC nerd, I'm continuously requesting stuff from Newegg.com - new parts, new parts, and other delightfully quirky stuff. The explanation I've been an unwavering Newegg client for a long time isn't simply the cost of the products (which is profoundly serious), yet rather the emphasis on client support and the subsequent cycle Newegg has set up.

Whenever I submit a request, I get definite rundowns of my buy (counting essential following data so I can hit "Revive" on the request page to see where my stuff is), as well as client care data, connections to applicable items I may be keen on, and a wide range of different assets. I'm provoked to leave surveys and criticism about my experience, urged to contact a genuine individual on the off chance that I have inquiries concerning my request, and could examine or respond to inquiries regarding my buy for different clients who are thinking about purchasing anything I just went a little overboard on. As a rule, it's simply an extraordinary shopping experience - which is the reason I've been purchasing my equipment from Newegg for a really long time.

Remember about your clients when they've given you their Visa subtleties. The more consideration you pay to them after they've purchased something, the more probable they are to turn out to be savagely steadfast brand evangelists who won't just transform into fulfilled recurrent clients, yet will likewise proceed to tell and their companions (and blog perusers) about how extraordinary you are. At the point when a client purchases something, offer them something free of charge (see tip #11). Converse with them via web-based entertainment (more on this right away). Send them a smart, helpful subsequent email with motivations to purchase from you once more. Anyway you get it done, cause your clients to feel like the priceless little snowflakes they are - think connections, not exchanges.

21. Nail Your Value Proposition - And Make It Immediately Obvious

Excessively many organizations lose deals and sit around idly by zeroing in on themselves. Recollect how we examined that individuals would rather not buy things, just take care of their concerns? Indeed, another difficult truth is that except if your clients are the brand evangelists we've been discussing, by far most of them couldn't care less about you or your organization - just how your items or administrations will improve their lives. For this reason your offer ought to become the overwhelming focus in the entirety of your advertising correspondence and site content.

Basically, your offer is the essential explanation clients ought to purchase from you, not your rivals, and the commitment of the worth possibilities will get by putting resources into anything that you're selling. Offers can be separated into three fundamental regions:

♦Importance: How your item/administration will take care of clients' concerns
♦Quantifiable worth: The particular advantages your item/administration offers
♦Differentiator: Why clients ought to purchase from you and not a contending organization

When you separate an incentive into these three parts, it turns out to be not difficult to see the reason why these components ought to illuminate basically all that about your promoting, informing and site content, from the duplicate on your landing page to the substance of your email showcasing efforts. Is there any valid reason why you wouldn't zero in solely on these parts of your items?

Investigate your point of arrival duplicate, deals guarantee, and other promotional materials. Is the offer promptly self-evident? On the off chance that not, now is the right time to return to the planning phase. All that your possibilities see ought to attach back to your offer somehow. The more noteworthy the apparent worth you can make encompassing your items or administrations, the more deals you'll make.

22. Utilize the Voice of the Customer for More Resonant Ad Campaigns

Ideally, you're now utilizing PPC and paid social to grow your span and track down new crowds. Be that as it may, the language you use in your missions can hugely affect your transformation rates (and, subsequently, your deals), so my fourth tip is to utilize "the voice of the client" in your missions - yet what's the significance here?

The voice of the client is a statistical surveying strategy that adjusts duplicates to the requirements, needs, trouble spots, assumptions, and revolutions of the shopper being focused on by that specific information. This interaction frequently incorporates language and stating utilized by clients themselves during statistical surveying and center gathering testing.

The model above, from bookkeeping programming organization FreshBooks, utilizes the voice of the client to extraordinary impact. During its statistical surveying, FreshBooks found that its objective market (entrepreneurs) viewed accounting as difficult and testing, thus it consolidated language utilized by its objective market in its informing.

This procedure can be uncommonly strong, as you're utilizing the specific stating utilized by your optimal clients to arrive at your optimal clients.

23. Pinpoint Your Best Attribution and Conversion Paths

Once in a while, it feels like you're doing everything right, just to see your change rates floating in the vicinity of "hopeless" and "pitiful." Oftentimes, this is nothing to do with the informing or situating of your promotions (however it pays to take a gander at this intently), yet rather a misconception of when and where transformations are going on.

One of the main things you ought to do assuming your change rates look low is to analyze your attribution models and transformation pathways in Analytics. You might be shocked to find that pieces of your showcasing methodology that seem like change duds really impact your web-based deals. For instance, perhaps natural hunt is certainly not an incredible channel for changing over into deals, however individuals who track down you first through natural pursuit, and afterward see a Facebook promotion are exceptionally similar to turning into a paying client. Assuming that is the situation, you ought to twofold down on satisfied showcasing and empty some cash into Facebook remarketing as well (see Tip #1, underneath).

24. All things considered Talk to Your Prospects on Social Media

Dynamic commitment with possibilities by means of web-based entertainment is ignored as a potential deals device by a wide margin an excessive number of organizations since it is seen as unimportantly affecting genuine deals - when as a matter of fact this is perhaps of the most effective way you can increment brand mindfulness, consumer loyalty, and deals.

Consider when you tweeted at an organization, or remarked on a brand's Facebook page - and the organization really answered you by and by. What impact did this have on your view of that brand? I'll bet it turned out to be altogether better. Giving quick, fair responses to questions that potential clients have about your contributions is an incredible method for expanding deals, as the more consideration you are seen as paying to possible clients, the more probable individuals are to need to purchase from you. This likewise brings about spontaneous social criticism among clients themselves - the sort of brand openness and "publicizing" you can't buy (indeed, not such that sounds authentic, at any rate).

25. Use Remarketing to Close Way More Deals
Regardless of whether you're running a PPC crusade or a Facebook promoting effort, any computerized showcasing drive takes time,

cash, and work to achieve. In the event that you're not utilizing remarketing, you're basically depending on imminent clients changing over right away, which never occurs (and is precisely just about as insane as it sounds).

www.ingramcontent.com/pod-product-compliance
Lightning Source LLC
Chambersburg PA
CBHW031513210526
45464CB00007B/2889